Awareness of Language

How Language Works
Barry Jones

We are always putting thoughts into words. But we do not often wonder how our words make sense to someone else. This book looks at how language works. It asks you to think about
- why we learn language
- what sorts of sounds we make
- what words are and how they fit together
- how language shows who things belong to
- how words show that there is more than one of something
- how to talk about the past and the future
- how the order of words helps us understand who is doing what to whom
- how to go about learning a foreign language

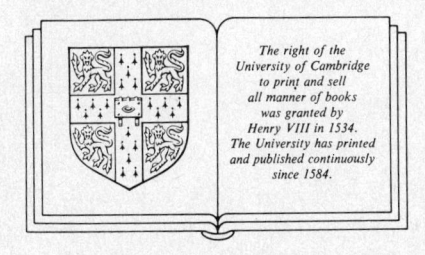

The right of the University of Cambridge to print and sell all manner of books was granted by Henry VIII in 1534. The University has printed and published continuously since 1584.

CAMBRIDGE UNIVERSITY PRESS

Cambridge
London   New York   New Rochelle
Melbourne   Sydney

1 Why do we learn language?

What is this baby telling you? The noise she is making is not just for fun. She cries and someone comes running. What does she want? We have to guess. But that's not always very difficult. When the baby wakes up we know she probably wants to be fed, so we feed her. We begin to learn how to interpret her cries as we get to know her better.

First few weeks...

What screams and shouts can do for you

What has the baby begun to discover by making noises? She sees that she can attract our attention. She cries and we feed her or pick her up. She is, in fact, learning how to communicate. This is her first step in developing her language, whatever language that may turn out to be.

As she gets a little older a baby begins to make a variety of sounds. Whether the baby is Japanese, Indian, Russian or English, most experts interested in language have found no differences in the sounds made during the first six months of her life between one language and another. No matter which country she lives in, when she is happy she coos! This sound, like her cries, produces an effect on those around her. They cuddle her, make soft noises, talk to her and play with her. She likes this so she does it again and gets even more attention. This kind of enjoyment and getting what she wants encourages her to make more sounds.

Next few weeks...

What coos can do for you

Not only can she get food as a result of her cries, she can also make people smile, talk to her and hold her. Her language of cooing builds up bonds between herself and other people. Together with her smiles and laughs, her language links her firmly to her family. Language is a means of making relationships with people.

and now if you would like to say a few words...

When a baby coos she makes sounds like 'Aaah' and 'Oooh'. Next she adds sounds like M, P, B, D. After about seven months a baby repeats sounds. She says things like 'Mama', 'Dada', 'Booboo'. When your mother and father heard you say 'Mama', and 'Dada' they were probably very pleased. Ask your parents if they remember what sounds you first made. Ask them also about your brothers or sisters.

2 All sorts of sounds

Children learn to make the sounds of the language spoken around them. A Chinese child in China, for example, learns that different sounds have different meanings. This is like English. He also learns that the high or low *note* on which one word is spoken can change its meaning. The arrows show whether the voice goes up or down.

Sound systems in action

The sound of the word *ma* in Chinese can mean several different things. It depends on which note or tone of voice is used.

If a child says *ma¹* (first tone)   it means an 'old woman'.
If he says *ma²* (second tone)   it means 'hemp'.
But if he says *ma³* (third tone)   it can mean a 'horse'.
If he uses *ma⁴* (fourth tone) it means 'to scold'.
These tones help to make meaning clear, for him. But we can hardly hear the difference between them!

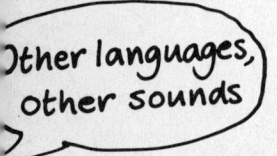

Why the Chinese use tones

but I wanted a horse!!

Other languages, other sounds

There are sounds in other languages which we do not have in English and sounds in English not to be found in other languages. African languages, like Xosha, have a 'click' in their range of sounds. Italians, Spaniards and Russians 'roll their Rs' like people speaking English with a Scottish accent.

S   The English R sound does not exist in many languages. So speakers of other languages find an R hard to say when they speak English. They use the nearest sound from their own language. For example, a Chinese person might use the L sound. How would you help someone make the R sound?

[S] Other sounds found in English which speakers of other languages find hard to make are the two different TH sounds, as in words like '*th*ink' and '*th*at'. How would you help someone make these sounds?

[G] If there are speakers of other languages in your class ask them to teach you to make some of the sounds of their language. In Punjabi there is a sound like a D followed quickly by a TH. You say the name 'Indra' as if it were written 'Ind(th)ra'.

ਇੰਦਰਾ

Sounds make messages

What do we mean when we say someone speaks English with a 'foreign accent'? Do you have a 'foreign accent'? Does anyone in your class have a 'foreign accent'? Which English sounds are hard for you or them to make? When we are learning another language we have to learn a lot of new sounds. Some are hard to make at first. Sometimes you feel a little silly trying to say them. You should not feel silly. Everyone needs a lot of practice before they get them absolutely right!

He's saying he wants a lightly boiled egg with some bread and butter and a mug of milk

BA!

Whatever his country of birth, a baby learns to talk like the people around him. Every child in every country knows that by making certain sounds he can get his message across to his listener. The different tones in Chinese are quite natural to a Chinese child. He would not get them right if they did not serve a purpose!

When you listen to a twelve-month-old child talking you find that you cannot understand everything he says. Sometimes he has a go at making a certain sound and he cannot manage it. He learns to make it in the end, when he is a little older. Or it may be that only his mother, father or sister can make out what he is saying. Only they can link the sound he makes to the thing or person he is thinking about.

First words

[S] Ask your family if they remember anything you or a brother or sister said when you were little which was not a 'proper' word – like 'dai' which one little English boy used to say for a 'wheelbarrow'. Why do you think you stopped using that word?

3 Words as labels

What does the word 'word' mean? Words are sounds with meanings that other people recognise.

Along the road comes something looking like this. How will you talk about it when someone asks you why you look surprised?

What you need to know is what name to give it. You want to be able to say something like:

'I have just seen a ? !'

If only you knew what name to give this funny creature you could talk about it so much more easily.

When you use the sound that everyone else uses then communication is easier. It's just like putting labels on things. If you don't use the same labels as everyone else you cannot easily communicate. For example, the following words are very common in the United States but some British people would not understand them: 'cookie', 'drapes', 'diaper', 'elevator', 'garbage'. In the same way an American might not understand what you meant if you talked about 'braces' (for holding trousers up!) or used the word 'lorry'. What words would an American use?

We call these 'label' words *nouns*. So 'road', for example, is a noun. 'China' or 'Daniel' which are names, are called 'proper nouns'. When you learn the labels that everyone else around you uses, then you can talk about particular things, or particular people or places.

5

Thank goodness for nouns

biscuits
tea
coffee
jam
butter
margarine
eggs
flour

Words and clues

P Here is a shopping list.

Try rewriting this list without actually using these words. Write a *description* of each item instead. Change the order of the items and see how quickly your friends can guess what you are describing. If the list had been more complicated (for example: digestive biscuits, self-raising flour, blackcurrant jam) you would have had an even harder job trying to describe each thing on the list.

Even to use only part of a word often does the trick. Part words like 'nana' said in a certain way, together with lots of pointing and waving arms, will probably get an English-speaking child a banana. Or perhaps his granny will come running! Or the child's words 'pane! pane!' might make his mother say 'Yes, there's a big blue plane, high up in the sky.' His mother does this because she knows what her child is talking about. She can tell from gestures (pointing and waving, for example) and from watching her baby learn other words, what he wants her to notice. She knows that his language, even at this early stage, is always surrounded by lots of clues as to what it means.

Some of the things which help us understand what is being said are:
   the tone of voice
   expressions on the face
   gestures
   what else is happening

Labelling the world another way

In some parts of the world, it is not always labels for things or people – nouns – which a child learns first. When we find out more about what children from other countries say when they learn to speak, we discover some differences. A Navajo Indian child in the United States, for example, according to some language experts, begins by talking about things *happening* around him. In order to share this experience with others, just like the little boy who kept saying 'pane' (or 'plane'), the Navajo child starts by using *verbs* (usually action words), not nouns. This is because, for the Navajo Indians, actions – like doing, moving, thinking, etc – are more important than things. Some people explain this by saying that the Navajo tribespeople think about life in a different way from Europeans. For these people understanding how the natural world *works* is the important thing, how things *happen*, what people *do*. They are not so concerned, as perhaps many of us are, with owning things.

There are other differences too, in the way children of other nationalities start to learn language. A young Yana Indian boy from Northern California in the United States, learns the word *bana* for 'deer', but his sister learns the word *ba*! *Both* words mean 'deer'. The one you use depends on whether *you* are a boy or a girl.

Another example from the same language is
  t'en'na if you are a boy and
  t'et if you are a girl.
Both words mean 'grizzly bear'!

Differences of these kinds show clearly that first steps in language, after the first six months or so, may be very varied. What, however, remains the same for every child in every country is the reason for learning to speak. At this age we all need language to describe the world around us, speak to other people and encourage our listeners to talk back to us. We need it, too, to help us feel safe and part of the world in which we live.

Sometimes the world is labelled differently according to the age of the person speaking. Show the pictures in the margin to your grandparents or elderly neighbours. Write down what they call each object. Do you use the same word?

S Sometimes the English used in the United States does not label the world in the same way as the English used in Britain. Look at these examples. Can you think of any more?

USA	GB
appartments to rent	flats to let
bathroom	toilet
trunk (of car)	boot
hood (of car)	bonnet
windshield (of car)	windscreen
muffler (of car)	silencer
sidewalk	pavement
principal	headmaster
drugstore	chemist
movie	film

S In this example spot *four* nouns:
- What did the barman say when a ghost asked for a whisky?
- 'We don't serve spirits.'

4 Words together

So far the language we have looked at has been mainly single sounds or words. But just as the child grows so does her need for more and more language. Just to talk about things, or people, or what's happening, is no longer enough. The child needs to say how one thing is linked to another, and how one person is linked to another. While listening to people talking children hear lots of separate words joined together. Soon they learn to join words together, too. It works better that way for getting what they want. It enables them to talk more about the world around them. If a child is given a plain biscuit, yet knows that delicious ones covered in thick chocolate exist, she quickly learns to put the word 'chocolate' with the word 'biscuit'. A German child would speak the words in the same order as the English, and say *Schlokoladenkeks*. A French boy or girl might say *biscuit au chocolat*. Each language has its own way of saying things.

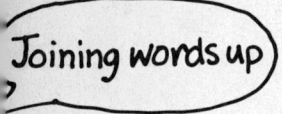

LELLO TRACTOR all gone...

Aged 1½–2

Joining words up

Chocolate biscuit! / biscuit au chocolat! / Schokoladen keks! / en chokolade kiks / रास्पबेरी चॉकलेट / बिस्कुट बिस्कुट

P Here is an example for you to try. It shows you how another language joins separate words together.

Have a go at writing an *Aztec* dialect. This will rely on you being able to spot the pattern.
(See next page.)

[P] Read these words carefully:

Aztec	English meaning
ikalwewe	big house
ikalsosol	old house
ikalcin	little house
komitwewe	big cooking pot
komitsosol	old cooking pot
petatwewe	big mat
petatsosol	old mat
petatcin	little mat
komitmeh	cooking pots
petatmeh	mats
koyamecin	little pig
koyamemeh	pigs

[P] 1. How does this language say 'big' and 'little'?
2. How does it show that there is more than one of something?
3. What does *sosol* show at the end of a word?
4. Now see if you can work out how to say:
   (a) little cooking pot
   (b) big pig
   (c) houses
   (d) old pig

(Adapted from Waldo E. Sweet: *Latin: a structural approach* University of Michigan Press.)

spot the pattern!

Aged 2–3

Now you know something about the way a language quite different from English puts words together. Each language has its own way of combining words, and its own patterns. When we learn a new language we learn not only new words and new sounds, but we also learn new patterns. We know that, if we follow the pattern, we will normally be understood.

Between the ages of two and three, as children are developing quickly and exploring more of the world around them, they need more language to describe what they are finding out. At this age they are probably saying words like 'all gone' when their cup of milk is empty. They learn quite quickly that the

same two words describe other situations. So from their first combination of words, perhaps 'milk all gone' – they go on, by following the pattern, to say:
  'tea all gone'
  'blue tractor all gone' or even
  'Daddy all gone'.
The child soon realises that the pattern can be made to fit all kinds of situations. This is an important step forward.

Daddy AllGone!

A French child discovers a different pattern. In French a two-year-old uses one word *fini* for things which have been 'finished', but a different word *parti* for people or things that have 'gone away'. A German child would use *aus* for anything 'finished', and *weg* for people or things that have gone away.

At this age children begin to put lots of words together. Sometimes, by listening carefully to what they say, we can find out which patterns they have already discovered and those they have not. Here is what a two-year-old boy said comparing a blue tractor and a red one on his grandfather's farm. He said:
  'Old blue tractor not exhaust pipe on.
  Grandpa's red tractor trailer on.'

Something new needs a new word

The little boy was quite fascinated by the different things he saw on the farm. Since this was a new and exciting experience for him he quickly learnt the names of what he saw. He wanted to talk about his discoveries to everyone he met. To do this he needed the words:

tractor	old
exhaust pipe	blue
trailer	red
on	Grandpa's

He also needed to be able to join all these words together to say what he wanted. This boy had reached a new and important stage in learning to speak. He was trying not only to put words together but also to put them together in the right order.

To be understood by other people we all need to join words together in an order that other people recognise. Words join together like jig-saw pieces. The pattern of the pieces helps us fit the words together. Sometimes, like the little boy talking about the tractors, we don't quite get it right. But even in the little boy's sentences the order is good enough for us to understand him.

Here are some experiments for you to try. Look at these six words:

[P] Dumpty sat Humpty a on wall

How many ways can you find to rearrange them so that they still make sense? Check your ideas with your partner. How many sentences have almost the same meaning?

[P] Read the following two phrases:
(a) *sea green*
(b) *green sea*

In phrase (a) what is being described, *sea* or *green*? And in sentence (b)? Do you all agree? What pattern have you discovered here?

[P] Fill in the gaps:
(a) *Ben is older . . . Jim*
(b) *You can have the sausages . . . are in the fridge.*
(c) *I love her . . . she is nice.*

In sentence (a) you have written *than*. How do I know what you have written?
In sentence (b) you have perhaps written *which* or *that*.
In sentence (c) there are several words which fit.
List what your friends have written. There won't be many to choose from. All these examples show how words fit together in patterns which we all know.

5 Nuts and bolts of language

Aged 2–3

A two- or three-year-old child builds up her language very quickly. She does this because she either needs or wants to talk. Here are just some of the bits of language that she is very good at using by her third birthday.

The child is beginning to find it useful to use words to point out the difference between things. A boy can ask for his 'blue train' rather than his 'red' one. A girl can get a 'big hammer' rather than a 'small' one. The words 'blue', 'red', 'big', 'small' enable us to pick out something special. They are called *adjectives*. Adjectives are useful words to learn.

In some languages people do not always use *adjectives* to draw attention to differences in the world around them. In the language the Eskimos speak there is a large number of *nouns* to describe what we simply call 'ice' or 'snow'. Differences of thickness, thinness, hardness or softness are not described by adjectives like 'thick', 'thin', 'hard', 'soft', and so on, but by a different word every time – a different noun. The meaning of each noun is very precise, too. If your life depends on knowing as much as possible about what the ice and snow around you is like, then it is not surprising that you make up a lot of different words to describe it. In warmer countries people don't need these words for ice and snow. That is why they don't exist in their languages.

Good and helpful are adjectives

He's hard of hearing

Up with Prepositions!

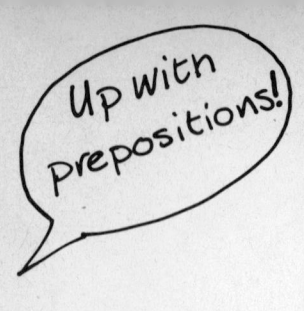

A two-year-old child needs to learn to talk about where things or people are. She has to learn words which show position – words like 'in', 'on', 'under', 'over'. These are called *prepositions*. The child needs words like this when she wants to be put onto a chair or to get her mother to put 'something *in* here'. She needs to show where things are, or where she wants them to be.

Prepositions really are very useful – for making things happen and for talking about things you cannot see. Imagine you are a Stone Age person; you have a cooking pot, a fire, some water and a Stone Age bison you have just killed. You are trying to tell your young Stone Age son what to do for dinner. It's no good just showing him (you have hurt your big toe out hunting and you can't move!). You have to tell him to pour the water *into* the pot, to put the pot *on* the fire and to put the chunks of meat *in* the water (*without* the help of Dad, but *with* the salt *under* the rock *at* the corner of the cave).

In English we need a lot of these kinds of short words. (They're called *pre*-positions because they come before the noun. *Pre* = Latin for 'before'.)

But not all languages use prepositions. So how do they manage to tell anyone to do something as simple as putting water into a pot? Finnish has a rather clever way; the Finnish language makes the ending of the *noun* different. Finnish has 15 of these different endings and no prepositions.

P In the riddles which follow find *five* adjectives:
1. *Question*: What is yellow and strong and jumps from cake to cake?
Answer: Tarzipan

2. *Question*: What is black and white and red all over?
Answer: A penguin with sunburn

[P] Here is a short story.

A spozzled girl opened the front door to her teacher.
'Are your grumpled parents in?' asked the bompy teacher.
'They was in,' said the spinny girl, 'but they is out now'.
'They *was* in! They *is* out!' exclaimed the boony teacher.
'Where is your grammar?'
'In the front room watching the telly.'

Replace the nonsense adjectives. Choose ones which make sense. Then compare notes with your classmates.

[P] What would be very difficult to talk about if there were no adjectives?

Try writing a short description of your bedroom using no adjectives. This will help you discover some part of the answer to the question.

[P] Now try writing a description of making a cup of tea with milk and sugar. Describe all the stages. Which prepositions do you need? Could you manage without them?

[P] Not all speakers of English use prepositions in quite the same way. What does an American mean when she says these things?
(a) 'The store is open Monday *through* Friday.'
(b) 'It's been nice meeting *with* you.'

6 Doing things to words

A two-year-old likes to talk about who owns things. This is why she says:
   Daddy's garage. Mary's book. Mummy's hairdryer.
A few months earlier she probably began by saying:
   Daddy garage. Mary book.

However, the words *Daddy garage* could have meant:
   Daddy, (go to the) garage! (an instruction)
   Daddy (is going to the) garage. (an observation made to someone else)
   Daddy('s) garage. (another observation)
   Daddy (is in the) garage. (a *different* observation)

Similar confusion occurs with the two words: *Mary book*
In order to make herself clear the child needs to add the *'s*
sound.

[S] What different things could she mean by *Mary book*?

Other languages do not always work like English. To show to
whom things belong in Chinese you add the sound *ti*:

人   *ren* is '(the) man'
人的   *ren de* is '(the) man's'

So the sentence in Chinese:

人的卡.   *ren de shu* means 'the man's book'.
我
我的   *wo* is 'I'
       wo de is 'my'

[S] What's the Chinese for 'my book'?

In Hindi to say 'Peter's car' you say *Peter of car*

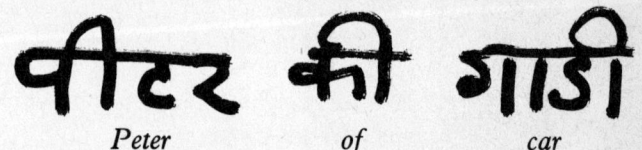

पीटर की गाडी

    Peter   *of*   *car*

A two-year-old child also begins to learn to talk about more
than one of something. She makes *plurals*. By two-and-a-half
most children are saying:

    one boat, two boat*s*
    one train, two train*s*
    one horse, two horse*s*

At this age she has often worked out that, to say 'two . . .' or
'lots of . . .' she might have to change the sound at the end of
the word which follows.

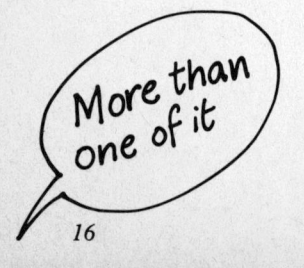

She is now beginning to discover more and more about *patterns* in language. Sometimes she makes words fit the wrong pattern. A two year old might say 'two mans', 'four sheeps'. It's easy to understand why the child is getting these plurals wrong. She has spotted one pattern and makes all words follow it. She has not realised yet that there are other possible patterns.

[S] Why do you think languages need ways of showing plurals?

[S] [P] Here are some common mistakes made by children learning to speak English. What should they say instead? Can you explain *why* they make each mistake?
  'There are two mouses.'
  'Look at those big gooses.'

To say 'two . . .' (of anything) in English is quite complicated. Do you realize that you need three different sounds: -ez, -z, -s?
  one *glass* : two *glasses* (-ez)   also *garages*, *bridges*
  one *card* : two *cards* (-z)   also *boys, cars*
  one *book* : two *books* (-s)   also *cliffs*

Don't forget the exceptions, when some words change some of their letters, for example:
  one *knife* : two *knives*
  one *hoof* : two _____

[P] Can you think of any others? Compare notes with your partner.

[P] People learning English sometimes find it difficult to know which sound they should add to make a word plural. How could you help them to get it right? Does there seem to be a rule?

[P] How many words can you think of that change their *sound* in the plural instead of just adding *s*?

Here is an example:
man - men
Now you try:
child - ?

P Some nouns are usually only known in the plural, words like: *scissors, clothes, jeans* etc. We don't talk about one scissor, or one jean, do we? How many more can you find?

S Read this story. There are 10 mistakes in it. How many of them can you spot?

A big, strong lion was out walking through the jungle. He came across two deers, three gooses, two ox and five doormouses. Suddenly he roared,
'Who is king of the jungle?'
Frightened, they all replied,
'You are, sir!'

Pleased with their answer, the lion went away. Later he saw a couple of calfs, cleaning their hoofs, three wolfs and their wifes, and four woolly sheeps. Approaching them silently from behind, he roared,
'Who is king of the jungle?'
'You are sir!' they all replied.
Again the lion went away pleased. Then he came across an elephant.
'Who is king of the jungle?' he bellowed.
Without a word the elephant picked him up in his trunk, threw him in the air, watched him land heavily on the ground, then jumped on him. The lion scraped himself slowly off the grasses and said:
'Alright, alright – there's no need to get mad just because you don't know the answer.'

If you speak German, you use different sounds, too, to make nouns plural.
1. Some words just add (*-e*) like this:
   das Boot – the boat   *die Boote* – the boats
2. Other words add (*-e*) and change the sound of the vowel in the middle:
   der Hut – the hat   *die Hüte* – the hats
3. Others add (*-n*) like:
   die Schule – the school   *die Schulen* – the schools

Try to make some German words plural. Use the pattern above.
1. *Das Spiel* – the game   *die* _____ – the games
2. *Der Sohn* – the son   *die* _____ – the sons
3. *Die Blume* – the flower   *die* _____ – the flowers

In Malay you just say the word twice when you mean more than one.
For example: *bunga* – flower   *bunga bunga* – flowers.
If *orang* – man how do you say 'men' in Malay?

7 Gender and what it does

Imagine you hear someone saying 'She likes ice cream'. You know that the person who likes ice cream is female. 'She' is perhaps a woman or a girl. The word 'she' tells you this. If a friend says, 'He is very clever', you know that 'he' means a male. The word 'it' normally means a 'thing'. For example, talking about a bicycle, you say, 'It's very dirty'. The words 'she', 'he' show the sex of a person. Sometimes we give a sex to some 'things'. Ships, cars, hurricanes, for example, are often 'she'. For most things, though, we say 'it'.

Some languages always give a sex to things as well as people. In French, all things are either 'she' or 'he'. The word for 'a book' in French is male. The French say *un livre*. 'A house' in French is *une maison*. The word *une maison* is female.

When we are talking about language we use special words. The special word we use for female words is *feminine*, and, for male words, *masculine*. We also say that masculine and feminine show the *gender* of a word.

This is a new idea for English-speaking people, since we do not usually give genders to nouns. French children, on the other hand, know that *all* nouns in their language must be either masculine or feminine. Italian and Spanish children are not taken by surprise by this when they learn French. Nouns

Answers: 1. *Die Spiele*, 2. *Die Söhne*, 3. *Die Blumen*

are masculine and feminine in Italian and Spanish, too. Spanish children put *el* or *un* before masculine nouns and talk about:

    el hijo – the son   *un hijo* – a son
    el burro – the donkey   *un burro* – a donkey
    el hombre – the man   *un hombre* – a man

Before feminine nouns there is *la* or *una*; so Spanish people talk about:

    la casa – the house   *una casa* – a house
    la canción – the song   *una canción* – a song

(There are other words for talking about more than one thing.)

If the name of a thing is feminine in Spanish or Italian, it is *usually* feminine in French too (Spanish: *la canción*   French: *la chanson*) and the same is true of masculine words (Italian: *il burro*   French: *le beurre*). Why do you think this is so?

In German, there are three kinds of nouns, masculine and feminine and *neuter*.

Der shows masculine:
der Mann – the man
der Junge – the boy
der Bleistift – the pencil

Die shows feminine:
die Frau – the woman
die Schule – the school
die Tanne – the fir tree

Das shows neuter:
das Mädchen – the girl
das Feuer – the fire
das Loch – the hole

For English speakers it does, at first, seem strange that 'girl' (*das Mädchen*) is *neuter*.

What we English-speakers would expect is that the gender shows the sex of the person. Here is a good example of where it certainly does not. The fact that *Mädchen* is neuter has to do with the last four letters -*chen*. These mean a *little* something; and words ending in -*chen* in German are always neuter.

Russian, too, has masculine, feminine and neuter words but uses a pattern of endings on the nouns to distinguish one from another.

In Punjabi it is not the nouns but the verbs which show masculine and feminine.
mā chulē = 'I am going' (a girl or a woman speaking)
mā chula = 'I am going' (a boy or man speaking)

We have seen that many languages work in similar ways to each other. Other languages work in quite different ways. Each, though, has its own system. English is only one system amongst many. But it is a system with its patterns and rules, just like all the others. Because languages have patterns and rules a child can learn a lot of language in a short time. After all, by the time you were four years old your language, (your mother tongue, that is), was already very like that of your parents. You were able to put words together so that you could, even then, talk about your needs, wants, ideas, thoughts and feelings.

It's a fact that, whatever your language is, you can usually speak it quite well by the time you are about four years old. You still have a lot of things to find out, though. Most people go on learning more about their mother tongue all their lives.

COME..DADA..MAMA! WALKIES!!

Oh I do wish they'd pull themselves together and begin to talk properly

P Dutch, like German, has three genders, masculine, feminine and neuter. The language has two words for 'the': *de* before masculine and feminine nouns and *het* in front of neuter nouns. Here is a short story in Dutch. See how much you understand.
1. First of all read it aloud to see if you can guess what any of it means.

De dag was koud. Er was sneeuw op de grond. Er was ijs op het meer. Er was en boot op het meer. Het huis was warm. Naast het vuur sliep een oude man. Hij had een rode kap op zijn hoofd en een lange witte baard. Een hond zat naast hem op de vloer.

2. Can you find the Dutch for any of these *adjectives* in the story: cold, old, warm, long, white, red?
3. Now find these *nouns*: snow, ice, sea, day, boat, house, fire, head, beard, dog, floor.
4. Now find these *prepositions*: on, by (next to).
5. In Dutch 'a boat' is *en boot*, and 'a man' is *een man*. Why do you think there are two ways of saying 'a'?
6. Does word order in Dutch seem different from English?
7. Now try to answer the following questions. Don't be afraid to guess!
   (a) What was there on the ground?
   (b) What was on the sea?
   (c) Was the house cold?
   (d) What was the old man doing?
   (e) What was on his head?
   (f) What was his beard like?
   (g) Where was his dog?

8 Talking about the past and future

One thing that you can do through language is to tell others what has happened and what is going to happen. Humans can actually talk about the past – what has been and gone – and about the future – what hasn't yet happened.

Between the ages of two and three most children want to talk about what *is* going on now, or about events which happen*ed* a little while ago. They like to say what they *are* doing, or what they *have* done during the day. It is important for them to be able to say whom they *have* just *seen* or what happen*ed* a few minutes ago.

Later on they get the idea of different points in the past and how far back something happened.

Your present Past and future

Tense?

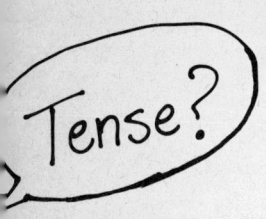

Words like:
  I have *just* . . .   or
  Three years *ago* . . .   or
  Yesterday . . .

help us to talk about the past. To say what we did we need to use a verb, and we need to use it in a particular *tense* (*tense* points to the time something happens: in the past, in the future, for example).

In English we can talk about the past in different ways. We sometimes make a difference between the way we describe something which happen*ed* quickly and something which *went on happening* for a long time.

In other languages. like French, the difference is *always* made clear by the verb endings, as you can see below. First read this paragraph in English:

'Kelly came in, sat down, opened his newspaper and began to read. He wore a yellow tie and had a red nose.'

Read that paragraph again.
What was the first thing that happened?
  Kelly came in.
And the second thing?
  He sat down.
And then?
  He opened his newspaper.
And then?
  He began to read.
And is the next thing that happened: he wore a yellow tie?
Obviously not.
And equally obviously the next thing that happened was not: he had a red nose.
Kelly had a red nose and wore a yellow tie *at the same time as* he came in, sat down, etc.

In French this difference between things that happen one after the other and things that happen at the same time as something else is shown by the forms of the verbs.

Kelly est entré, s'est assis, a ouvert son journal et a commencé à lire. Il portait une cravate jaune et il avait le nez rouge.

Kelly did not come in reading his newspaper, but the *-ait* ending shows that he did come in wearing a yellow tie and with his usual red nose. This *-ait* ending can also be *-aient*,

-ais, -ions, -iez according to who or what it is agreeing with.
Kelly prenait un bain quand le téléphone a sonné.

The *-ait* ending shows that Kelly's bath was going on at the same time as the telephone rang. So the sentence must mean:
'Kelly was taking a bath when the telephone rang.'

And it can not mean:
'Kelly took a bath and then the telephone rang.'
Differences like that can be quite important.
(From: B. Page and A. Moys *Lire*)

Sorting out the past

Each language has its own ways of sorting out differences of this kind. These differences are marked by different patterns of sounds. In English one pattern is often:
'I -ed' or 'I -t' (*past tense*)

[P] We say, for example, 'She usually *works* a seven-hour day but yesterday she *worked* only five hours.'
'Worked' shows the thing happened in the past. It is the *past tense* of the verb 'work'.

Write out these sentences and fill in the gaps using the following verbs in the *past tense:* stay, play, ask.
1. Last year I . . . in the school football team.
2. They . . . if they could go out.
3. She . . . all day.

[P] Not all verbs in English follow this pattern though. Can you correct these things that a two-year-old boy said?
1. I eated two sausages for dinner.
2. That little boy goed home on his bike.
3. He seed it.
4. I taked the dog out.

[P] American English mostly makes the past tense in a similar way to British English. Americans do say, however,
'He *has gotten* fat.'
How would you say the same thing?

Children sometimes get the verb forms wrong – in exactly the same way as they get plurals wrong and say 'sheeps' instead of 'sheep'. At first they see a pattern and make all verbs fit it. Then they learn that some verbs do not follow the pattern.

Here are three more examples from a two-year-old boy's conversation:

Daniel fall*ed* down in the deep sea.
Mummy tear*ed* paper.
Man runn*ed* fast, very fast.

They show him trying to sort out the right form of the past tense. He has discovered the pattern which forms this tense: *-ed* or *-t*. But he still has to learn that some verbs don't work that way. He has to learn that:

'fell' is the past tense of 'fall'
'tore' is the past tense of 'tear'
'ran' is the past tense of 'run'

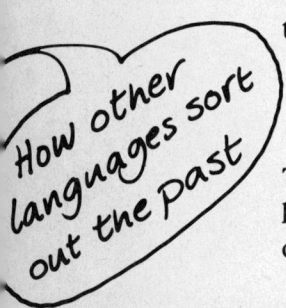

How other languages sort out the past

These kinds of sound patterns in verbs differ from language to language. Let's look at what an English sentence becomes in other languages. Look at the verbs.

English: Daniel *has fallen* into the sea.
French: Daniel *est tombé* dans la mer.
German: Daniel *ist* ins Meer *gefallen*.

French has *-é* as one of the ways it marks the past. Other endings may be *-i* or *-u*.

German uses *ge* in front of the verb to mark it.

Russian, too, uses letters in front of the verbs not at the end. Chinese adds another *word* to show that the verb is past tense, like this:

wo he – 'I drink'
wo hele – 'I drink have' = I drank
wo heguo – 'I drink have' (a long while ago)

我 喝
我 喝了
我 喝过

[P] The English *past tense* can sometimes be difficult to get right if you are learning English. To help a foreigner, see if you can jot down the words missing from the list below:

Here is an example:

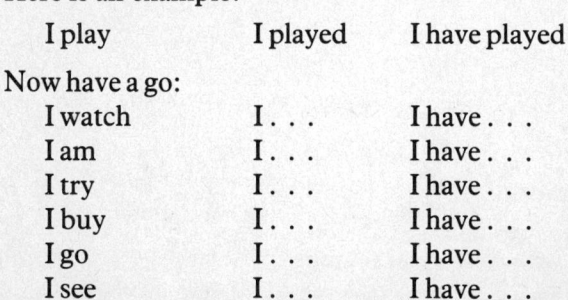

| I play | I played | I have played |

Now have a go:

I watch	I...	I have...
I am	I...	I have...
I try	I...	I have...
I buy	I...	I have...
I go	I...	I have...
I see	I...	I have...

I sit	I . . .	I have . . .
I do	I . . .	I have . . .
I eat	I . . .	I have . . .
I think	I . . .	I have . . .
I sing	I . . .	I have . . .

There are lots more – 68 in all! Can you think of some?

Do you think English is easy to learn? What makes it easy and what makes it difficult?

9 Everything in its place?

Have you noticed that you put words together in an order which keeps your meaning clear. This explains how you can understand both these sentences:

    Man bites dog.   Dog bites man.

The subject does it all!

The only difference between them is the word order. How does it change the meaning? The order of the words tells you who is doing the biting! The do-er is called the *subject* and the person/thing at the other end of the action is called the *object*.

[S] Here are some jumbled sentences:
1. his Matthew bicycle rode new
2. kicked the goalkeeper the ball
3. band number one played the hit their
4. chased the dog the girl

Rewrite them in an order which makes sense.

(a) In some sentences were there different ways of putting the words together?
(b) Underline the *subject* of each verb.
In a different colour underline the *object*.
Which always comes first?

(c) Underline the *verbs* in a different colour.
   Where is the verb in each sentence?
The sentence looks like this:
   subject+verb+object
   Man   bites dog.
This is the word order of a very large number of the sentences that you say every day. However, the order of words is not always a foolproof guide as to who does what. You might have a subject at the end of a sentence like this:
   Into the plains rode the 5th Cavalry.

[S] Try an experiment to prove to yourself what a help word order is in sorting out meaning. Here are three nonsense words: *chinzle dinzle minzle*
You have no idea what they mean. Read this and see if you can answer the questions.

   The dinzles are minzling the chinzles.

1. Who or what is doing something?
2. What are they doing?
3. Who are they doing it to? How can you tell?
4. Which word is the subject?
5. Which is the verb?
6. Which word is the object?

Here is another sentence: *Oh, minzle the dinzles and the chinzles!*

1. Who or what is going to be minzled now?
2. Does this sentence have a subject?
3. Who or what is the object?

Many languages use: *subject+verb+object* as their favourite combination of words. Here are some examples from Chinese:

wo ai ni means 'I love you'

我 爱 你

ni ai wo means 'you love me.'

你 爱 我

I sing in Italian, Spanish and Russian

This is almost the same pattern as in English. Can you spot the one thing that is different about the Chinese pattern? Other languages work in other ways. Some languages combine subject and verb into one word.

| English = | I sing | he sings | Spanish= | canto | canta |
| Italian = | canto | canta | Russian= | po'ju | po'jot |

As she grows older, to learn more about the world around her, a child must ask questions. She might need to know *where* something is – like her toys or her drinking mug – or *when* Daddy or Mummy is coming home. Later she will want to know *why* things are as they are. Question words, in English, usually come at the beginning of a sentence.

'*Where* is my jacket?'
'*When* does the bus go?'
'*Why* are you jumping up and down?'

Questions, questions, questions.

Let's look at ways an English speaker learns to ask other kinds of questions. Again the order of words can be very important and it forms a pattern. Here are some examples in English:

Will you close the door?   Have you seen him?
Are you coming?   Did the elephant drink the water?

One way other languages make questions is by changing the order of the words, too.

French: *Viens-tu?* – are you coming?
(come you)
German: *Kommst du?* – are you coming?
(come you)
Chinese: *Ni lai bu lai* – are you coming?
(you come not come)   你来不来

说 S   The Chinese for 'speak' is *shuo*, so the Chinese for 'Do you speak Chinese?' is
ni shuo bu shuo zhongguo hua?   你说不说中国话

1. Which words mean 'Chinese'?
2. The Chinese for 'understand' is *dong*. What's the 懂 Chinese for 'Do you understand Chinese?'

Changing your tone of voice means something

In French, German and English you can also ask questions by changing your tone of voice. If you raise the tone of your voice you are asking a question.

You are coming?   Tu viens?   Du kommst?

Stress and what it does for you

P This use of the voice – changing the tone – is another way of changing the meaning of the words we use. We can change our meaning by stressing different words. Say these sentences aloud asking a friend to stress one of the words in italics. How does this change the meaning?

Go in *there alone*? Never in a million years!
I *never* want to see *you* again!
Do *you eat seaweed*?
Do *you* have a *cat*?

All of these show how our tone of voice tells someone, amongst other things, whether we are surprised, impatient, annoyed, pleased, or just believe what we have been told.

How many different meanings can you give to the following sentences by changing the tone of your voice?

Where do you think you're going?
Who has eaten my sweets?
Paul asked Tom to go to the shops.

10 Getting by in a foreign language

Have you any foreign language needs?

So far in this book we have looked at what you did when you were small, learning to speak your own language. Do you remember if it was difficult? Did you have to try very hard? Probably you remember nothing about it.

Now imagine you have won a three-week holiday in a foreign country of your choice. What bits of the foreign language do you think you would need, or want, to know? You might choose to go to Spain. Expect everyone around you to speak only Spanish. What should you learn?

Sort out where you might find yourself

First you need a list of some of the things you might be doing. Look at this check-list of possible places to go, or where you might find yourself.

street	bus-stop	station	café
shop	boat	airport	restaurant
campsite	bus	post office	
hotel	train		Any more?

What you might have to say

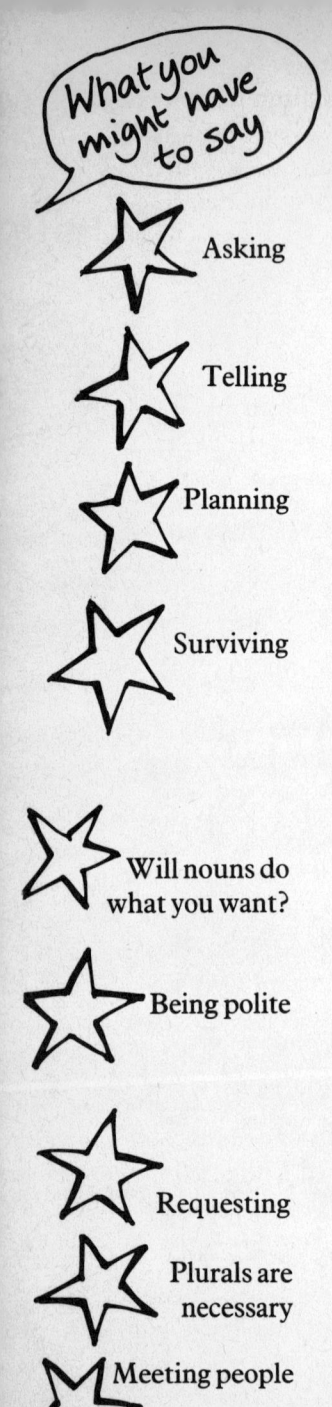

Try now to decide what you would want to do or say. Here are some ideas.

★ Asking

You probably want to *ask* for:
 directions and about prices
 information about places to see, where to go for amusement, etc

★ Telling

You may want to tell someone:
 information about yourself
 what you like and don't like

★ Planning

You might also want to:
 give (and maybe refuse) invitations
 make plans, etc

★ Surviving

When you arrive you will have to buy food and drink, and find a place to stay or you won't survive for long! When you were young you had the same need for food and drink. Is the language you should learn the same as the language you used as a small child? How did you ask for food and drink? Will the same kind of language help in a foreign country?

★ Will nouns do what you want?

Let's look as a simple example. You could learn a list of *nouns* (names for things). This is a little like a baby labelling his world. When a one-year-old wants a banana he might just say the one word 'banana' and get what he wants. He knows only single words. When you are in a foreign country if you say just the one word 'sandwich' you, too, may get what you want. But it helps if you can say a bit more. You need a little more language to help you be polite, like the word for 'please'.

★ Being polite

★ Requesting

It helps to know:
 how to greet someone you don't know
 how to thank someone and say goodbye
It's also useful to know how to say, for example, 'Have you any . . .?' 'I would like some . . .'

★ Plurals are necessary

It also helps to discover how Spanish shows plurals, because, sometimes, you'll want more than one thing.

★ Meeting people

As soon as you start meeting people you may want to say some simple things about yourself. You may also want to find out something about the people you meet. This means, perhaps,

★ Talking about yourself

★ Saying what you like doing

you will want to say what your name is, where you come from, what you like and don't like doing. You might also want to say something about your family, interests and hobbies and, maybe, favourite sports. You can, no doubt, add a few more ideas yourself. To do all of this you will need to use verbs in the *present tense*. This lets you talk about what you *usually do* or what you *are doing*.

You need verbs desperately

S Write six sentences about yourself, your family, your interests, where you live. Underline the *verbs* you have used. Are they all in the *present tense*?

You can get quite a long way with verbs in the present tense only. But very soon you may find that you want to say something about your plans.

S What do you think you'll be doing this weekend? Write down four sentences about what you're going to do.

To talk about your plans you will probably have begun each sentence with 'I will . . .' or 'I'll . . .', or 'I'm going to . . .'. Have you done this? You'll need to be able to say what you're *going* to do.

You're likely, too, to want to talk about what you've done. So you'll need the *past tense*.

S Now write four sentences about what you did yesterday. Underline the verbs you have used. Are they all in the past tense?

These three tenses are all very useful. There's no rule, though, that tells you in which order you should learn them. See what you think after you have read the story which follows:

An American language expert, called Robert Dato, who studies how we learn a foreign language, once conducted an interesting experiment. He and his family went to live in Madrid, the capital of Spain. Their young son knew no Spanish when he arrived. So, to see how he got on when he was with other Spanish children, his father put a microphone on his son's belt. In this way he was able to record the Spanish his son used over a period of 12 months. He was especially interested in the parts of verbs his son used. This is roughly the order of what the boy learned to say.

1. **Commands**	Look!	*Mira!*
	Come!	*Ven!*
2. **Present tense**	You have (+noun)	*Tienes . . .*
	I don't have (+noun)	*No tengo . . .*
	There's (e.g. There's no television)	*Hay . . .* *(No hay televisión)*
3. **Immediate future tense**	I'm going to (+verb)	*Voy a . . .*
4. **Past tense**	I have . . . (e.g. *I have lost* my money)	*(He perdido el dinero)*
	He has . . . (e.g. Miguel *has broken* the bottle)	*(Miguel ha roto la botella)*
5. **Imperfect tense**	We were (e.g. We *were* in school	*(Estábamos en el colegio)*
	You *had* to (+verb) (e.g. You had to write this for me)	*Me tenías que escribir ésto*
6. **Future tense**	I'll (+verb) (e.g. I'll show it to you	*(Te lo enseñaré)*

If you begin learning a foreign language this list seems to be a reasonable guide to the order of tenses you might need to learn. Everything the American boy said was only learnt because he wanted to communicate with others. He was speaking because he wanted to get along with those he met. What about you? If you were in Spain you too would need food, drink and shelter – and you'd want to make friends.

Language helps make friends